The Serpentine is delighted to present this exhibition, which is Leckey's first solo presentation in a public gallery in the UK. We are enormously grateful to Mark Leckey for accepting our invitation and for his enthusiasm for this project from the outset. We could not have asked for a more engaged and thoughtful collaborator and it has been an immense pleasure to work with him to realise this show. We are also indebted to him for generously producing two Limited Editions on the occasion of this exhibition and for allowing the Serpentine to benefit from their sale.

We would like to warmly thank Samsung, who have kindly provided a range of equipment for *GreenScreenRefrigeratorAction*. *The Independent* is the Gallery's Media Partner this summer and our thanks to Simon Kelner, David Lister and Petra Luckman for bringing the Serpentine's programme to a larger audience. We are also indebted to Charles Asprey and to Marlon Abela for their generous support of the exhibition's opening celebrations. The Council of the Serpentine Gallery is critical to the Gallery's success is innumerable ways and we are enormously grateful to its members, as well as to our Patrons, Future Contemporaries and Benefactors, whose continued support plays a vital role in enabling the Serpentine to deliver all of its programmes.

This exhibition would not have been possible without the generosity of lenders who have agred to share works from their collections. Charles Asprey, Boros Collection, Berlin; Fondation Louis Vuitton pour la création and Keith Wilson have supported the exhibition in this important way. The Henry Moore Foundation has lent a Henry Moore bronze to the exhibition and has been tremendously generous with material from their archives. We would like to thank Richard Calvocoressi, Director, Anita Feldman Bennet, Head of Collections and Exhibitions, and Suzanne Eustace and Claire Smith, Assistant Curators, for their assistance.

We have benefited considerably from the advice and expertise provided by James Mullord and we thank him for playing such a pivotal role throughout the planning stages of this project. We also greatly appreciate the guidance and support we have received from Mark Leckey's representatives, Martin McGeown and Andrew Wheatley of Cabinet Gallery, London, Gavin Brown and Lucy Chadwick at Gavin Brown's enterprise, New York, and Daniel Buchholz and Christopher Müller at Galerie Daniel Buchholz, Cologne and Berlin.

We are delighted to include texts by the artist as well as by Neil Mulholland, Simon Reynolds and Catherine Wood. We are grateful for the continued support of Koenig Books, London, who collaborate with us on the Gallery's publications. This catalogue has been designed by Fraser Muggeridge studio in close collaboration with the artist and our thanks go to Fraser Muggeridge, Stephen Barrett and Joseph Hales for their skill in making this book.

Finally, we would like to acknowledge the team at the Serpentine who have produced this exhibition. Kathryn Rattee, Exhibition Curator, Mike Gaughan, Gallery Manager, Claire Feeley, Assistant Curator, Sally Tallant, Head of Programmes, and Nicola Lees, Public Programme Curator, have worked closely with the wider team to realise this project and we thank them for their enthusiasm and commitment.

Julia Peyton-Jones
Director, Serpentine Gallery and
Co-Director, Exhibitions & Programmes

Hans Ulrich Obrist
Co-Director, Exhibitions & Programmes and
Director, International Projects

Fiorucci Made Me Hardcore

DIRECTORS' FOREWORD

SEE, WE ASSEMBLE is a new exhibition developed with the Serpentine Gallery by Mark Leckey. In a multi-disciplinary practice that encompasses sculpture, sound, film and performance, Leckey explores the potential of the human imagination to appropriate and to animate a concept, an object or an environment. Drawing on his personal experiences as a London-based artist, who spent his formative years in the north of England, Leckey returns frequently to ideas of desire and transformation in his work.

This exhibition has been selected to represent the most significant developments in Leckey's practice. This group of works spans the breadth of his career, from the moment Leckey first gained international recognition in the late 1990s to the present, and points towards key themes in his work. Leckey's keen interest in sculpture, his nostalgia for dying elements of British pop culture, his exploration of the affective power of images and his nuanced understanding of the impact of networks and technology on culture are all signalled here. Conceived as a series of immersive spaces, the installations respond to the Serpentine's unique architecture, acoustics and location within Kensington Gardens.

Meticulously sourced and reconfigured archival footage is a feature of the earliest work on show, *Fiorucci Made Me Hardcore*, 1999. One of Leckey's best-known works, *Fiorucci* is a visual essay on the history of underground dance culture in the UK during a period from the mid-1970s to the early 1990s. Leckey sourced documentary imagery over a two-year period and the film is notable both for its remarkable soundtrack, which Leckey made using the sampling techniques that grew out of the scene depicted in the film, and its nostalgic, elegiac tone, which is amplified by the grainy, low-fi quality of the original material.

Leckey's *Sound Systems*, large, functioning stacks of speakers, are another point of connection to music and club culture but they also speak of the artist's desire to continually activate his works and the spaces they inhabit. Two of the *Sound Systems* are installed in the Serpentine's largest central space opposite a towering Henry Moore bronze entitled *Upright Motive No. 9*, 1979. These works are brought together for *BigBoxStatueAction*, 2003–11, in which Leckey establishes a dialogue between the two imposing sculptures. In a series of performances that will take place during the exhibition, Leckey will play a sound piece created for the Moore work. Leckey sets up a relationship between these two seemingly disparate sculptures, corresponding directly with the Henry Moore work in order to coax it to reveal its 'thoughts' and its history.

GreenScreenRefrigeratorAction expands on this desire to give a voice to objects that are not typically heard. In this work, which centres around a black Samsung refrigerator, Leckey seeks to communicate the inner life of a 'smart' fridge – one that keeps an electronic tally of its contents. Responding to the idea that we are increasingly surrounded by technology, that it has created an ambient field around us, Leckey explores the possibility that we can be in constant communication with every aspect of our environment, that everything from sculptures to refrigerators is alive.

Leckey has also made a series of posters and a 'trailer' for this exhibition. Representing the 'brands' associated with the three main works on display, Fiorucci, Henry Moore and Samsung, these posters acknowledge and explore the transformative impact that brands can have on individuals as well as the role they play within wider culture.

THEY BURN SO BRIGHT WHILST YOU CAN ONLY WONDER WHY:
WATCHING *FIORUCCI MADE ME HARDCORE*

There are a number of angles from which you could watch Mark Leckey's extraordinary *Fiorucci Made Me Hardcore*. There's the anthropological view, which would see the footage of UK dance scenes as depicting not so much subcultures as cults: upsurges of the sacred within an otherwise brutally disenchanted and secularised post-industrial Britain, mystical youth tribes each organised around an array of fetishes, totems and rites. Such an analysis might zoom in on the parallels between Sufi whirling dervishes and the twirling dancers at Northern Soul temple Wigan Casino: each displays the same defiance of gravity and weightless levitation above the mundane. Or it might note the messianic fervour of sayings like Northern Soul's 'Keep the Faith' or rave's 'Hardcore Will Never Die'.

Another potential prism for *Fiorucci* is subcultural theory, the Marxism-influenced school of 'resistance through rituals' research that emerged in Britain during the 1970s. Here the focus would be less on transcendence than on what was being transcended: the alchemical synergy of style, music and drugs as a 'solution' to the impasses of the class system, a jamming of symbolic codes that achieved a kind of victory over the fate otherwise laid out for these working-class youths, while at the same time diverting them from pursuing a real and permanent solution to their problems through political activity.

Other readings could draw on more recent and trendier theories. For instance, a Lacan/ Kristeva/Bataille analysis that would be more, well...analytic, in the Freudian sense, citing notions like 'drive' and the 'acephalic' in order to bring out the elements of repetition and regression in these drugs-and-dance cults, with their fixated trances and autistic-seeming bodily movements of rocking, shaking and twitching. Or perhaps we could adopt a cybernetic approach, influenced equally by Deleuze & Guattari, Brian Eno and Kodwo Eshun, and examining these subcultures in terms of machinic energy, the feedback loops of 'scenius', the generation of posthuman intensities and so forth.

All these angles have their strengths and virtues; all make visible certain aspects of Northern Soul, the Casuals and Hardcore Rave (the three separate but linked subcultures with which *Fiorucci* works) while inevitably obscuring others. My own reading would probably touch on all of these approaches at various points, but would betray a pronounced slant towards paradox, looking at the way in which these cults are dedicated to beauty and elegance yet so often produce grotesquerie and indignity, or at how these movements based around perpetual motion seem to find their truest essence in moments of stasis, frozen poses, tableaux. I expect that I would find myself drawn irresistibly towards oxymoronic formulations: the dance subculture as an exit that becomes a dead end, offering transcendence that turns into a trap, achieving a triumph that is simultaneously a form of defeat...

But there's something a little too neat and tidy about these formulations, a faint taint of smugness, which may well be unavoidable but still feels inadequate. All these different ways of dissecting/contextualising/historicising the strange subcultural blooms of a Britain that has disappeared never to return, however well-intended they may be, serve ultimately to explain away and domesticate these unassimilable phenomena. In so far as they successfully translate these cults into other terms (the jargons of particular discourses and disciplines) such readings deflect you from the singular power of Leckey's artwork:

its reality, the fact that it is made almost entirely of salvaged documentary footage. Now, obviously the material has been processed: it's been selected out of a much larger mass, it's been juxtaposed and sequenced and altered in various ways (mostly within the domain of time and speed – slowing down, freeze-framing). The footage fragments have also been severed from whatever original audio track they possessed and given a new one (a remarkable piece of sound art in its own right). But despite this working up of the material, in a certain crucial way the ultimate effect is of an artist who doesn't get in the way of the raw material, out of respect. What comes across is the palpable reality of what you are looking at, in all its absurdity, monstrosity and glory. There is an opacity to the found material, an insistent but mute materiality: limb-dislocating contortions, foetus-pale flesh, eyes vacant in trance or stiletto-sharp with vigilant pride, maniacal smiles that split apart the dead grey mask of English 'mustn't grumble' mundanity, faces disfigured with bliss.

At times, the sensation of watching *Fiorucci* borders on invasive: obscene not in the porno sense (staged, graphic, every detail exposed by the bright light) but obscene as in the more murky and partial view of the peeping Tom or eavesdropper. It can feel a little like what looking at covert videos of people masturbating might be like: their expressions and sounds and fantasy murmurings. You sometimes think: this should really never have been filmed, these moments should really never have been captured, these are secrets that should really never have been shown. Because all this really happened. This is how some young people actually spent their time, this is the thing to which they devoted all their energy and money and passion and life-force. Leckey has pieced together a kind of shrine made up of sacred relics, fragments of nights that the participants may barely remember, image debris from a time in their lives that they might conceivably regret, for any number of reasons, or, perhaps worse, might regret because that time is long gone, is passed and past. What you are witnessing – what Leckey is re-presenting here almost without comment – is no less than a collection of what may have been the best moments of a number of young British lives in the last three decades of the twentieth century. Their finest hour.

Simon Reynolds

Youths hanging out on the Ford Estate, Birkenhead, 1981

From *Happy Daze: A Personal Insight into the Acid House Era*

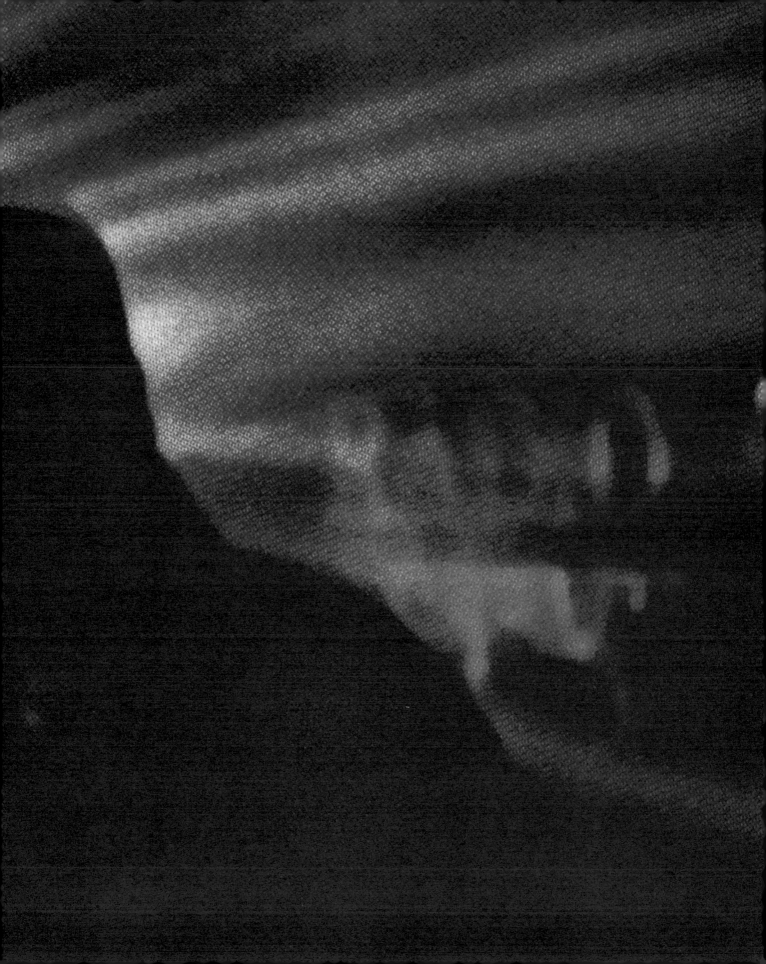

Capture your cherished moments on VHS cassettes from the days we travelled the orbital and no town, field or warehouse was safe.

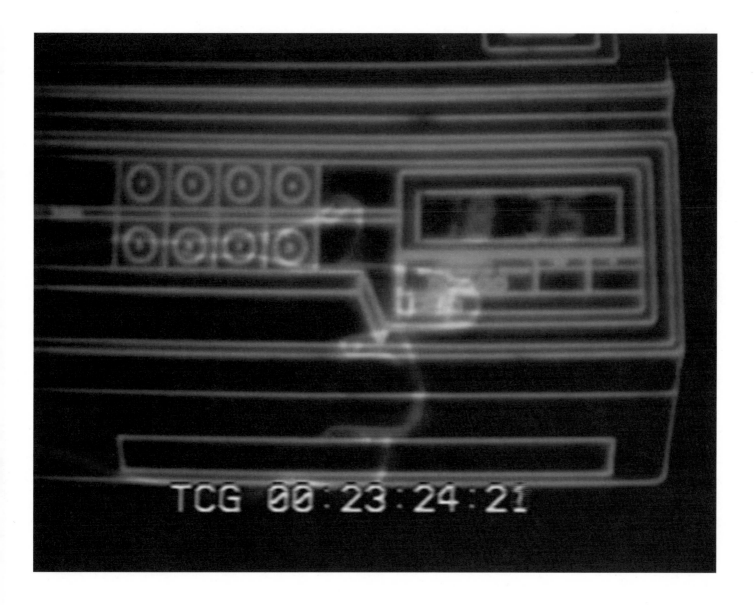

BigBoxStatueAction

Flyer for *BigBoxStatueAction*, 2003

A *Soundsystem* and Epstein's sculpture *Jacob and the Angel*, 1946 at the heart of the museum, after hours. Ten feet apart and matched on plinths across the Octagon, the plywood box and alabaster block made for a pleasing, unexpected symmetry. A crowd of faces concentrating inwards formed a circular fortress around them, sheltered in turn by the museum's fat stone columns and flat sandstone walls. Everywhere beyond that centre point – charged and live – was empty and dark and silent. Footsteps and voices skidded an echoing distance against the long sweep of polished marble floors. We were permitted into an illicit but protected place.

The *Soundsystem* spoke first, babbling its curious runic mouthings: Ddadadadaaaaaaaaa ... Mmnnnnouuummm ... Onammmouuuuuuuoo ... like the first utterances of a new-born thing, but ancient and found. Melodies and snatched rhythms crept up sliding scales, starting here and there, sometimes falling back into a melancholic minor, but then building slowly, with anticipation, and more slow still (Persuasion). And seductively. A man (Ed Laliq) sang high notes, near falsetto, but tempered by flatness, a bit off-key. A woman (Lucy McKenzie) appeared like a William Blake angel playing a trumpet-clarinet. And there was the realness and thereness of Leckey's own spoken voice (Persuasion).

The *Soundsystem*'s volume rose, and rose, and swelled, and filled the space so full that it threatened to burst open the sculpture's veined, flesh-pink alabaster skin, exploding its voluptuous solidity into mist in an ecstatic blast of sound. It seemed that the glass from the roof might simultaneously shatter at high pitch, and rain tinkling down.

We were temporarily inflated by this thought as we held our breath, collectively. Jacob and the Angel clung to each other, desperately tight. But instead of perpetrating violence, the *Soundsystem*'s music slid sideways into swe-e-et messianic sweetness, sweeping the crowd heavenwards, momentarily, to the thrill of an impossible dizzy peak. Then it shrivelled in a split second, as if someone had brutally yanked out the electricity.

* * *

After, in the new quiet, the museum and its objects looked unchanged. But atom by atom, molecule by molecule, the edifice, in its entirety, had been destructed. Re-made. Cold cut stone warmed and glowed and became tender with love. The circle of witnesses felt as solid as Stonehenge. An osmotic transubstantiation of people and music and matter, *BigBoxStatueAction* made, within the museum's walls, another kind of place for art. It was that place's summoning, and its memorial: a soft monument.

(Persuasion).

Catherine Wood

BigBoxStatueAction, 2003

Sound System, 2007

Henry Moore, *Crowd Looking at a Tied-Up Object*, 1942

Unveiling in May 1956 of Henry Moore's *Harlow Family Group*, 1954–55

Henry Moore, *Upright Motive No. 9,* 1979

BruderKriegSoundSystem, 2011

MY ODOODEM

First written for *BRUDERKRIEGSOUNDSYSTEM* at the ICA, London, 13 January, 2011. The following was to be read out at the beginning of the performance:

I am here to introduce the *Sound System* which like all systems is an ensemble: an ensemble is both a group of performers and it is a co-ordinated set of furniture, a unit of complimentary parts that all contribute to a single effect, the properties of which are determined by the behaviour of its constituents.

And these constituents are made up of the Treble, the Mid and the Bass.

The Treble carries the upper frequencies, those nearest the edge of hearing. Transmissions that are high above us in the yellow hills over 16,000 cycles. The unearthly pitch beyond the planet's boundary layer, the whistle of red sprites, the static of solar activity and the celestial speech of Enochian. The language of Angels.

The formation below the Treble is the Mid Range, the region where the most fundamental sounds lie: those familiar tones that are upon the Earth – or rather – between the Earth itself and the Heavens up above. This is the AND, the sound of AND, the AND between Up AND Down, Above AND Below, Upstairs AND Downstairs, Deep down in the sea AND Way up in the sky.

Underneath is the Bottom End: the subterranean forces below the Earth. The infra sound. The register of Caves and Crevasses where bodies of air move back and forth, back and forth, generating oscillating waves of pressure that vibrate the atmosphere.

Making it HEAVY

This heavy atmosphere is palpable, almost visible, like ectoplasm. Grey globs of foreboding oozing out of each orifice of the medium's body. A deep dread in the pit of the stomach rumbles and growls. The Borborygmus speaks. For these are the voices of the dead who have taken up residence in its gut. And through a form of gastromancy, the ventriloquist – me – can interpret these sounds. So that this colossal doll, this wooden dummy with all its interchangeable parts, can speak on my behalf, give me a voice with which I can address the public. A Public Address System that enhances and extends my tiny voice like a giant prosthesis.

But this doll, for all its parts, is headless. It is acephelous – an Organisation without a Head. A Corporation without a Chief. An Institution without a Director. A Realm without a Crown.

So although it is stacked vertically it is actually better seen *horizontally* – for there is no hierarchy to these parts. There is no low man on the Totem Pole. Each box is interdependent on another box. Again, it is a system and the defining characteristic of a system emerges from the interaction of all of its parts. Speech, for instance is not the product of the larynx, or lips or lungs or tongue or brain but the interaction between the whole. The whole body, the *BigBox*.

And this system here includes the human as well as the non-human. That's what a *Sound System* is. A unit of complimentary parts that all contribute to a single effect. It is brought into being through our affinities to one another, through our kinship. And this object is the totem of that kinship – a dodem – this is our dodem, my nin-dodem, you have your dodem and there are other o-dodem.

Unlike the Graven Idol that makes a lot of empty noise the Totem is not hollow, nor is it a silent thing that can only be held in private, like a fetish. The Totem is a collective representation in sculptural form brought out to mark occasions and events...like this one. It is a made thing that has taken on independent life, a machine that appears to have created itself.

Within it is held all the sounds of our ancestors, the talking drum, the church organ, the player piano and the 808.

So let the *BigBox* speak.

Mark Leckey

Promotional image for Jack Too Jack

INTERVIEW WITH MARK LECKEY
BY JULIA PEYTON-JONES
AND HANS ULRICH OBRIST

Hans Ulrich Obrist: If we look at your CV and your trajectory, you pop up in the early 90s, the same moment as the yBas – you were in the show *New Contemporaries* with Damien Hirst in 1990. And then there is an interesting moment when you stopped exhibiting and seemed to incubate for almost ten years, and then all of a sudden in 1999 you appeared with a masterpiece, *Fiorucci Made Me Hardcore*. Before we talk about this piece, which is perhaps the beginning of the show here, I'd like to ask about this early work? And I am particularly curious about what happened inbetween these two poles, about what you did throughout the 1990s, after you showed what you referred to as your Neo-Geo work?

Mark Leckey: I was up in Newcastle, at Newcastle Polytechnic. I was struggling to make work; I didn't know what I wanted to do. When I first went to college, I went there to make murals, I was obsessed with Diego Rivera. I wanted to make populist art. I was very suspicious of pretentious and over-intellectualised art. I wanted to make art that was accessible to everyone, I guess. When I got to college that became very difficult. I couldn't find a language, a satisfactory language to make work like that. I think I did what most students do, I looked to what was happening, to what was hip and at that time it was a kind of Neo-Geo thing. The work I made then is rubbish and I don't know why I got into the New Contemporaries with it. I was up in Newcastle in my second year when that work was selected. I just got lucky really. I'd made this piece of work and was put next to Damien Hirst but there was no connection between me and him or between me and anyone in that show.

I was on the selection panel for the New Contemporaries recently and now you don't get many students outside of London who actually get in because the disparity between the work is so great. There are not many people who get in from the provinces. But before it was different. 1989 was a very different place in the art world; it's not how it is today.

To answer the second part of the question, I had no sense of a career or that I even wanted to carry on making art. At that time I'd just been to art college and I had gone for numerous reasons. One being that I wanted to be in a band as much as I wanted to make art. I just wanted to be somewhere where there was a creative culture and art school seemed the best place to do that. Being at art school hadn't made me any more certain that being an artist was what I wanted to do; in fact it made me go the other way, it turned me off. It was a time when they introduced Maoist year zero to critical theory. There was no schooling in that before, no one was really aware of any of this stuff, especially up in Newcastle. You were completely unaware of French thought and suddenly it's dumped on you. And there was an expectation that you'd understand it, which I still find insane. The idea that students of 19 are meant to be *au fait* with Kant and be able to understand very complicated ideas about language. I still find it strange that that is part of art education now. I think it can really strangle you. Basically you either learn to speak that language, which takes a lot of dedication and time, or you don't. And if you don't, then you're not part of the discourse and you can't engage.

Julia Peyton-Jones: It must have been interesting going into that kind of realm and context. You went from one way of looking at the world to another extreme. I was wondering if maybe your interest in bands and music was perhaps a type of call to arms. As music is so prevalent in your works, whether this idea might be a fundamental part of your work?

ML: A call to arms? That's a good question. Maybe, possibly, I hadn't thought about it like that. I've always thought that what I do is very particular to me. I don't think of it as being universal in any way. I always try and make work that is local to my environment. I guess I was looking for some kind of language that could exist outside of the institutions. I guess I am still interested in something that can do that, something that can have an effect beyond the quite narrow margins of the art world. To return to your question, Hans, in those ten years before I made *Fiorucci*, that's really what I was looking for, I was looking for a way of responding to the world. Trying to find something I could make, to find a language of communication. I just happened to alight back on art because it was the most welcoming and nurturing – partly because of people I knew, to be honest. I met Gavin Brown in New York and I was just hanging around the gallery with Gavin, like some Factory leech. And in the end he just persuaded me to make something really. So it came from my relationship with him more than anything else.

JPJ: And what role did nostalgia play in *Fiorucci*?

ML: I was living in America and I think it was a combination of the age I was then, I was in my late 20s, and of being away from home, being away from the UK, it just ramped up this nostalgia for my past and for an idea of British pop culture, which was slipping away. Basically I always think that if there is a call to arms, it's to do with the idea that I belong to the end of something. It's like I'm the last of the twentieth century and we're at this pivotal moment, this transitional moment where one century dies and one century begins. It feels like I am full of possibilities but also full of things that are in decay. When I look at *Fiorucci* now, it feels like a ghost film. It was meant to be a celebration of life and vitality, but there's something haunted about the whole thing. There's something ghostly about it.

HUO: It is now a piece that influences many artists, especially those who are maybe 10 or 15 years younger than you. How did *Fiorucci* come about? Who influenced you at that time?

ML: The main influence on me at that time, that gave me a structural way to make it, was Johan Grimonprez. His work *Dial H-I-S-T-O-R-Y*, 1997, had a massive influence on me when I saw it. And when I was in San Francisco, there was this guy called Craig Baldwin who works at this place Artists' Television Access and he makes what he calls cargo cuts, which are based around this idea of found footage. *Fiorucci* is about the culture of the used, sampling. All the music is made through sampling and through those kinds of techniques. So I wasn't really thinking about it in an art way, in terms of those kinds of precedents, although obviously the more you learn the more you realise that they're already implicated in it. My understanding of sampling and appropriation came more from music.

Initially I wanted to make an essay about recorded moments in pop culture, recorded video moments. That sounds really clumsy, but I was interested in performances captured on video, where the potential of pop is realised. The magic of pop when it's caught by video, that was what it was going to be and then I struggled with it. It wasn't working and so I just kept having to adapt and change it. I was making this documentary and it had this distance to it, this disinterest. I was really disappointed. The more I worked on it, the more involved I got with it and the more I considered it to be a language that I could speak, something that I had an experience of. I wanted to be immersed in it.

It was a very weird process making *Fiorucci* and it set me off on everything I did since. It's still the way I make work – I discovered a way to work with images, to work with video in the making of that film. Images have an incredible effect on me.

I had this sort of sickness while I was making the film. I was sick with nostalgia and I'd find this stuff quite upsetting, it was almost unbearable just to sit and watch this stuff again. A lot of the time I'd be editing drunk. It was like being drunk and looking at old photographs of a lost love. I'd just be really sentimental about the stuff. So I guess that was what this film was about, a kind of mourning, an elegy for these lost moments, this lost time. But it was also about realising that the actual material of the images has a power in itself, like the grain of video and the more deteriorated, the more generational loss has taken place, the more effective it becomes. The actual look of the film, the video, has this power to amplify those feelings of remembrance, memory and loss.

JPJ: The role of branding also seems to be an important point both in *Fiorucci* but also in your work related to Casuals and, possibly more recently, with *GreenScreen*. Can you tell us what interests you about brands? Is it what they stand for? Or is it a way of reflecting the culture of our times? If you go back to a refrigerator of the 1950s, for example, you don't need to see any other pictures, you've got the image of that period in your mind. What is it that interests you about brands?

ML: I guess it's what you've just said – brands imprint themselves on your psyche. They're just sort of there. I share brands as much as I share archaeology and ancient sites. Those two things are what make me up. You know brands are like the air that I breathe, I'm saturated with them. It seems impossible not to acknowledge them, but not in any kind of critical way. *Fiorucci Made Me Hardcore* basically says that a brand made me transcendent. That's what I meant by that title. Investing in something that was meant to be trite and throw-away made me more than I ever could be.

There's a direction that I feel you're pushed into in the art world, which says that any work that gets made automatically offers up an implicit critique of capitalism. I'm not sure what my critique of capitalism is. I'm not sure how critical I am of it in the end. All of this stuff

Photograph of Mark Leckey in 1984, Ellesmere Port, Merseyside

is a process of trying to understand the world through making work. Using these brands is a way of figuring out what my relationship is to these things – what they do to me and how they affect me. They're powerful things. But at the same time they magic up these things that are incredibly beautiful. Or that can be used in a way that is transformative. So I guess the simple answer is, when I use that stuff it's because I'm very ambivalent about it. I don't know what its power is and I can't just be critical of it because it's part of the fabric of the world I live in. I don't know how to step beyond that wall or be detached from it.

HUO: You have often been described as a *flâneur*. In an article for *Artforum* in 2002, Matthew Higgs compares you to Constantin Guys, Baudelaire's famed 'painter of modern life'. Higgs writes that 'only the sophisticated artist-flâneur, blessed, as Balzac determined, with superior insight, was able to truly experience the chaotic splendour of metropolitan hubris'. Would you say that this relationship to the *flâneur* is still relevant to your practice now?

ML: Less so. It's that dandy thing: as soon as someone says you're a dandy you want to reject the label. It's not a label that I ever wanted to wear. Sometimes I look at *Parade*, 2003, and I don't know if it feels too explicit in that sense. There's something that I do like about *Parade*, which is that it's very claustrophobic and sickly. And that's always what *flâneurism* brings to mind with me, it's a kind of bachelor sickness. I don't find it a particularly healthy mode of being. It's cut off from the world, cut off from real relations in the world, even though it purports to be about being in the world. I think it's about being in yourself, about making yourself into a machine. There's something very mechanical about it. When I was making that work that's what I wanted to be, I wanted to be a machine. I wanted to be this bachelor machine. I wanted to have that kind of production. But now I look back on it and it just seems very limiting. It's about reducing your world rather than expanding it.

Flâneurism is about sickness – the *Fleurs du Mal* – maybe I am still sick with the world, I don't know. I mean *GreenScreenRefrigerator* is a kind of sickness with the world, I guess. There's something about just you and a fridge and somehow believing that you can have a relationship with this thing, I think there's a *flâneur* aspect to that. If you go out looking at the world in terms of seeking objects that you can respond to and looking for objects that give up something about the

Parade, 2003 (still), DVD, 32 min

world, that tell you secrets about the way the world is, then you can become too close to objects and you can start misunderstanding objects as surrogates for other things, for real relations.

JPJ: It occurs to me that the whole idea of the *flâneur* is also about display. It's very performative in that way. You really embrace performance in your work and use it to a very sophisticated extent. Moving on from the display of a *flâneur* to the display of technology, what interests you about that? Is it something about our time, specifically our culture right now?

ML: Yes it's about our time, but I think it's also about how transformative technology is. Writing is a form of technology. We're technological beings. This is what we do, this is what we are. We use tools and that's what makes us human. We're surrounded by technology now, we live in an ambient environment, technology is creating this field, this visual and audio field. But I'm also interested in technology just in terms of art, in the effects that it has upon making work. The idea with the fridge is that it's a sculpture to me, but it's a sculpture that can talk. So what happens to sculpture once it stops being a dumb thing and it can respond to you? That seems like a massive change to me. It's an enormous paradigm shift. We're no longer about making things, making objects, we have to see objects in terms of some other kind of relationship to ourselves, more as something that we share the world with.

HUO: That's interesting because it leads us to your *Sound Systems*, which talk to us. You made *Parade* in 2003 and the *BigBox* performance incorporating your *Sound Systems* was also started in the same year. I was curious because these works have accompanied you now for eight years. This Serpentine exhibition, which isn't a survey or a retrospective, is your first monographic institutional exhibition in the UK and it includes work from 1999 to 2011. In a sense we could say that the *Sound Systems* are perhaps in some way an umbilical cord in your practice. At the Serpentine they are in the central room, which is always the heart of any exhibition. They are the only work that you have continued to make throughout your trajectory. How did they start – what was the epiphany or trigger for the *Sound Systems* and *BigBox* performances? And how do they evolve and change? Will they ever stop or will they continue as long as you work?

Sound System, 2002

ML: Hopefully they will continue. The problem if you make videos is that they can become so dead in a way. A friend of mine makes websites and they have this term for when information can no longer be interacted with, they call it 'dead media'. When something is online, it's kind of alive in that you can make constant changes to it. If it's printed out as a hard copy it's inert, it's immutable. So if it becomes a video then it's dead media. You end up at this final point, this finished point and I don't really want to make work like that. I want the stuff that I make to be there to be used so that I can use it again. And I think with the *Sound Systems*, I can use them again and again. They can be put into different situations and they can do different things. They're basically just a big surrogate voice box.

HUO: We had many conversations about what sculpture should go with the *Sound Systems* for *BigBoxStatueAction*. And in the end you went for Henry Moore's *Upright Motive No. 9*.

ML: And I'm glad it's a Henry Moore. The more I think about it the better it is. For one, he's British, which I think is important. It's got a relationship to this Gallery and he's like a brand himself.[1] He is as ubiquitous as Samsung. Everyone knows who Moore is and I think it's good for the show that you've got Samsung, Moore and Fiorucci, these three labels. Henry Moore's almost got his own font, his own brand design. I think *BigBox* needs something equivalent to the volume, to the mass of the *Sound Systems*. I'm looking for something monumental that I can have a conversation with. I guess the *Sound Systems* feel like a giant ventriloquist's dummy, but then I'm not sure which one's the dummy and which one's the ventriloquist. It's a means of communicating because if I just stood in front of the statue and tried to talk to it there would be something feeble about it. I don't think the statue would pay me any attention. I think it needs something that it can respect, that is equally as awesome as the statue to respond to it. So it's about these two giants talking to each other.

JPJ: What was really fascinating about the conversations that led us to Henry Moore was your forensic knowledge of British art, including names that are known to really relatively few people. What is it that has made you interested to become so well informed about the history of British sculpture?

Henry Moore, *Upright Motive No. 9*, 1979

1. The exhibition *Henry Moore at the Serpentine* (1 July – 8 October, 1978) marked the artist's 80th birthday and included work installed in the Serpentine's galleries as well as at nine sites in Kensington Gardens.

ML: For one I think that sculpture is what I do. I wouldn't like to say I'm a sculptor – that would seem too much. But I think I'm in that field and I try to understand that field as much as I can. It's the field that interests me most out of all the arts, even more than video or film, although it's really a toss up between the two. So it's just a desire for knowledge, a need to know what that stuff is and what it does and how it works. It's like discovering William Tucker. I only discovered him a year or two ago and I just read his book *The Language of Sculpture* and there's a whole other realm of knowledge there that can be used. Essentially I'm a magpie; I look to this stuff to steal from it or to absorb it. Everything is used for my own purposes. I don't know if knowledge can come from another place than that, but that's certainly what it is for me. I just need to know so I can use it. It's material.

JPJ: The interesting thing about those artists is that they are neither fashionable nor necessarily timely. They are very often forgotten and the fact that they are overlooked makes them all the more fascinating to revisit.

ML: I like archives, I'm interested in looking at archives and if you look at archives of British art you realise that you will soon join those archives and maybe not in the best possible way. You look at this stuff and think that could have been my equivalent back then. I could have been so and so from the 1960s and where is he now? I guess it's twofold, when you look at an archive you're looking at things because you want this information about what they are but also as soon as you start looking at them as an archive then they become something else, which is like *Fiorucci*. Archives themselves have their particular quality and you can get wrapped up in that and the information can become secondary. The form takes over from the content.

The March of the Big White Barbarians, 2005 (stills), DVD, 5.04 min

HUO: I also wanted to ask about your interest in public sculpture in London, which is the subject of your work *March of the Big White Barbarians*, 2005.

ML: Once you start to really look at public sculptures they're mysterious, they're oddly alien. They have a history you can read – not only the history of sculpture but also the history of art's relationship to culture and what people believed it could once do, which a lot of the time I now find quite alien. We are borrowing a Henry Moore work for *BigBoxStatueAction* in this exhibition and I don't know what I think of Henry Moore, I find the works weirdly foreign. But the process of doing this is about trying to find out if I do actually like it. The more I think about *BigBox*, the more I think it's a better form of art criticism. Instead of writing about a work, you set up a relationship with it where you can try and correspond with it directly and see what it has to offer. So at the end of this I might like the Moore, which is what happened with the Jacob Epstein sculpture I worked with when I did *BigBox* at Tate Britain in 2003 – I grew to really appreciate Epstein. So I might grow to like Moore or I might still feel indifferent to him.

HUO: From the beginning when we spoke to you about this exhibition, you said you wanted things to be activated on a weekly basis. The *GreenScreen RefrigeratorAction* is a work you are showing here for the first time in Europe. I'm very interested in hearing more about *GreenScreen* as an action, the action as a general principle for the show and the desire for this kind of unmediated experience in the age of the internet, which seems to get stronger again. Matthew Barney once spoke about performance in terms of a desire for unmediated experience.

ML: It's not unmediated experience. I guess that's the point: it's you in media. They're not performances in the sense of a return to a natural state or something more primal. I'm not saying that performances have to be like that. My performances are about your relationship to media and how your body is within that. With *Fiorucci*, you hear me mumbling drunkenly in the background sometimes. I left that in so that I'm there in the making of this thing. There's something about making video that I find weirdly tactile, although tactile seems entirely the wrong word. There's something about the relationship to your hand in the making of this thing – it's like working with an instrument, which I find quite confusing. Like your body is somehow confused about its relationship with this thing that you're looking at and this space that you should be able to enter but you can't. The more time you spend with it, the more you feel you're incorporated into it.

So I guess with *GreenScreenRefrigeratorAction*, it's just taking that idea to its conclusion. I get to be in the film like Mike TV in *Willy Wonka and the Chocolate Factory*. You're there in it and the thing with green screen technology is that it allows me to do that. It allows me to be literally in the media. There's me and the fridge, the fridge is an object and we're both these solid things but then the output is a two-dimensional

GreenScreenRefrigeratorAction, 2010

image where we're both on the same plane. We're both within this screen. In a dumb way I wanted to get as near as I possibly could to feeling what a fridge feels like, by taking the same chemicals as it does and just being in the same space as it is with nothing else surrounding it. So I can just have this correspondence with it. It's the same with *BigBox* actually, it's trying to know something. It's about suspension, about things being frozen. Like the fridge, the Henry Moore statue is a frozen image. *Fiorucci* is a lot about literally freeze-framing things, stopping images so you can suspend them and get closer to them. I guess that's the thing with all of this stuff, I want to get closer to these things and to know them entirely because they have such a power over me and I want to understand what that power is. That was what I was thinking about with this show, how everything is in this state of suspended animation.

HUO: It would be great to hear about the other actions that you have planned for the show.

ML: I'm going to do four performances of *BigBox StatueAction* and each one of those is going to be different. For one I might get the band up, Jack Too Jack, I might get them to do a performance. On top of that, I'd like to come in and just do things, impromptu talks. I always wanted to make a piece of work that I can leave in a gallery somewhere and feel like I'm there as well. Like it's a surrogate of mine and I get to be there in that space for the duration. I guess with this show it gives me the opportunity to actually physically do that. To come in and spend some time in the gallery. So I think maybe what I'll do is come in and start talking to people about what I thought the work was. That's how I want to do this show. I guess it's about distance again in that I don't want it to be distanced. I'm going to write the wall text and just explain to people why I did it rather than try to give some kind of overview. And I like the idea of just coming in and telling people face to face why I've done it.

JPJ: It's also something about getting to know your own work again in a completely different context. Because that type of knowledge through proximity over time seems to be a very important aspect of what you do. You distanced yourself somewhat from *Fiorucci* and then gradually you have come back to it. And maybe this show will allow you an opportunity to really fully embrace it in a different way once again.

ML: Yes, I think that's a good point.

JPJ: One of the fascinating things for the public is to see what an artist looks like. Being an artist is the most difficult job on the planet, in my view, and yet it is also perceived as a very glamorous job. So if you're generous enough to share that with people then it's an incredible opportunity for them and also for the institution. When the show is finished, what would you like to have happened, what would you like to have come out of it? What will make it different to other shows?

ML: Blimey, you can't ask me that. I find that really hard to answer because I have such disgusting ambitions for myself that I don't want to reveal them. One of the things that I find quite hard, actually – well not hard but difficult to get a sense of – is the need to please people in terms of making work. I try not to but I'm very anxious about the desire to be adored. So when you ask me a question like that, that's the first thing I think of. When you ask me what I want, if I'm honest, I'd say I want to be adored. It's something I need to find a distance from. I don't think it's useful or productive. I mean the thing about all this stuff, and realising this while talking to you as well, is that basically I'm just ravenous, I'm hungry for stuff. My desires have no limits – they just want, I just want. I'm like this wanting machine and so what I want in terms of my career I find that quite frightening because it's useful to make work with. The thing about the Samsung fridge and about Henry Moore is that I want both of them equally. I desire them both equally and that's what *Fiorucci* is also about, it's about desire. Sometimes I wish that I could put that persona away and not be so greedy in my every day life.

JPJ: Except it fuels ambition and I wonder if the desire that you've expressed to develop an art-related variety show, whether that's part and parcel of the same kind of thing?

ML: Maybe, but it's also part of what we were talking about at the beginning, about trying to find a more democratic language. The other thing that connects all the works in this show is the idea of giving a voice to things that normally aren't necessarily heard. *Fiorucci* is the most obvious case. It's about a class that dandifies itself in order to be acknowledged. The fridge is an inanimate object that finds a voice in order to change its status into something that we can more readily accept. I'm thinking of giving this show a title. And the working title I've got at the moment is *All my Aspirations*.

Someone asked me if *BigBoxStatueAction* was supposed to be tongue in cheek and this really goes back to your last question about what I want to come out of this project. It would be good if, at the end of this show, I had convinced people that these works are not tongue in cheek. I don't just look at these things as cool pop or something. They're necessary to me, they're extensions of myself. And it might look a bit stupid to have a fridge sitting there talking, but to me it's a real possibility that I have to engage with. It's not a critique, I'm not taking the piss in any way. It's what I believe the world is and I need to respond to these things. They are things that I aspire to and they in turn aspire themselves. It's my history, I'm lower middle class, upper working class, a child of Thatcher, I aspire. It's the ravenous appetite.

HUO: When I read things you have said or written, I often need a dictionary, which is interesting. For example, I am fascinated by your use of the word stigmergy. Are these neologisms or are they rare words?

ML: Stigmergy is an unusual word, it's from biology. It's what social insects like ants and termites do when they go out foraging for food or to find another nest. They leave a trail of pheromones and other ants then follow that trail and over time that trail gets built up and built up, eventually literally leaving a mark. It's a term that is now also used in computing. It comes from open source computing and it basically means you leave a mark for others to follow. It's the same idea that I was talking about earlier with 'dead media'.

JPJ: So it's about traffic in the broadest sense?

ML: It is about traffic in that sense, but for me it's an idea. The way it's used in computing means that nothing is original. The first mark may have been laid but no one knows by who. All these people have worked on it and it becomes this thing and no one knows who the author is. No one knows what the origins were and I like that.

HUO: We haven't spoken about your lectures yet in relation to your teaching. Can you talk about the lecture as a format? And I'm interested in your writing too. What is your relationship to language and to writing?

ML: The lectures came about when I was teaching at the Städelschule in Frankfurt. Teaching was quite confusing, especially in that school because the questions that the

Cinema-in-the-Round, 2008 (stills), DVD, 42 min

7 Windmill Street W1

Mark Leckey in the Long Tail, 2009

students ask, and the question of the school in some sense, is what is art's purpose? What are its functions? Everyone wanted to understand the epistemology or the ontological questions of art making. Usually, when you're in your studio, you're not really thinking too much about that stuff but when you're teaching and especially in an environment like that, then you're forever thinking about the market and the institutions and all the rest of it. So the lectures were a way of being able to talk about things, to talk about those kinds of questions in a very broad way. It was something I needed to do, just to get them out of my system. They were surplus to a work and I couldn't make a work out of them because they were too enormous, so I just had to put them into a lecture.

JPJ: It's interesting that you're making this exhibition for the Serpentine at a time when your own working conditions are changing. You're no longer working out of your studio in Windmill Street, which has appeared in several of your works. So what does it mean to lose a studio, on one hand, and what opportunities does that open up that haven't existed before?

ML: Well to lose it goes back to what we were saying earlier about the *flâneur* and the bachelor. That flat was my bachelor machine. I believed in that flat as a means of production, as a machine to produce things. I was very cut off and isolated in there and I could get completely immersed in what I did. I've given that up now because I didn't want to be that way anymore, mainly because I found someone that I wanted to be with and I didn't want to be on my own anymore. And also I think with these lectures, *The Long Tail* especially, it's like I said before, I want my mind to go elsewhere. There was something about *The Long Tail* that had an almost cosmic potential for me and I wanted to follow that trail. I think that the things that we can know about the world now just seem infinitely vast to me and obviously they were forever so but I guess through making art it's opened things up and they just keep opening up and opening up. Where I was before didn't allow for that, it was a very closed environment. I want to live more in the world than in my head.

JPJ: And live with your public by being here during the show.

ML: Yes.

HUO: Julia alluded to your plans for a TV show, an unrealised project, but do you have any other unrealised projects?

ML: I do, yes. I was going to say I want to make a film, but I don't want to make a film, I want to make something much more expansive. The thing about the lectures is what we were just talking about, this idea of a public performance and to keep expanding that out and make it more ambitious. Sometimes when I go to galleries, when I go on a gallery safari, I do look at a lot of art and think this is very limiting. It can seem quite reduced. I'm looking for something that's out in the world. I see art galleries as a sort of kernel and I'm not dismissing them but I want to move out from it. So I want to make some sort of film but then I'd like to make something online that functions as an online art work. Something you can put out there that works in this stigmergic way that I was talking about earlier. You put something there and then people can maybe develop it and then you come back and develop it and it's just this ever-growing, ever-changing thing. It's finding a way of making something that isn't authored in that way, but then it's getting people to find that place and become interested in it.

The Variety Show could be online and the film could be online. They could exist out there, it's just another form of distribution and I think it should be embraced. I don't know if I entirely believe in participation as an artist, it's got a lot of problems if you try and think about how people participate. But if you look at *Fiorucci*, it's about things generating themselves and the great thing about what you see in *Fiorucci* is that there is no DJ there, there's no one even running the clubs. They just come together through a group mind and the internet is that same kind of group mind idea realised. But that's so antithetical to the way that art gets made now. I don't know how to join the two things up. Talking about branding you know, I could become a brand and one way of getting people to go online is to follow your brand. But then that is a complete contradiction to the idea of not having a DJ, so I don't know...

HUO: We haven't asked you yet about your heroes. In previous interviews you have mentioned Jeff Koons.

ML: I'm a little ambivalent about Koons. I find him endlessly interesting but I don't know if I could call him a hero. What I like about him is that he offers an idea of art that is social, that exists in a social, participatory way

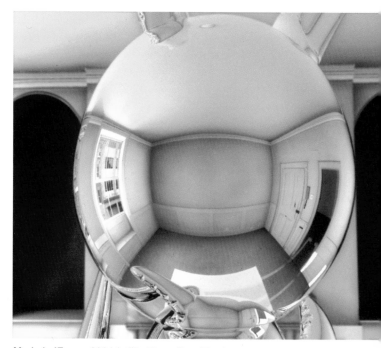

Made in 'Eaven, 2004 (still), 16mm film, 20 min

without having to get involved with relational aesthetics. It's just objects. I like what he says about this stuff, that he sees them as these secular objects that have this cultural, societal function. I find that really interesting. In terms of art heroes, Mike Kelley is definitely one. He's a big one. Richard Hamilton I like a lot. I like Francis Picabia, and going further back than that, Manet is my absolute hero.

He's the painter of modern life, isn't he? I just find it hard to think that in 100 or so years ago nothing has topped that. His painting *A Bar at the Folies-Bergère* (1882) as an image of modern life, it's just about the modernity of things. Koons' *Rabbit* (1986) gets close to it. I mean I could put those two works together, I think they do the same thing in some ways. Manet's is a century-old image that still seems totally about this age. Manet more than anyone else I think changed the way art was going. Warhol is a not-so-good Manet. *A Bar at the Folies-Bergère* is a reflective piece, it's totally about reflections. There's this idea that I think appeals to certain painters that you could just paint money, literally make a painting of a bill and, somehow, *A Bar at the Folies-Bergère* is a painting of money and all the things that money is. There are only a few works that have done that – Warhol has done it, Koons has done it. There we go, that would be my ambition – to make a work that is all those things and that reflects what it is. It shows desire and it is desire. It shows money and it is money. It's the thing itself, which is what I think is great about those works.

JPJ: You've also mentioned that the artist is present in those works and so you too would have to be present as the kind of impresario figure, the conductor of the orchestra.

ML: Yeah but I don't think of it like that. I'm not that figure, it's more just that I'm in it. I'm there, I'm implicated, it's not made by anyone else but me. It's that thing of not having a distance from it. I'm not like the Wizard of Oz, it's just like putting your hand print on something and saying I was here, I made this. But this is the contradiction I have at the heart of what I do. That I believe art has to come from some lived, personal experience but at the same time I want it to be this stigmergic process that has no room at all for the individual hand. I don't know.

HUO: And do you still draw or paint? Or is it Lee Healey who draws for you?

Poster for *Gorgeousness & Gorgeosity*, 2005

45

ML: Lee draws for me. It's that thing I've been mentioning all the way through, it's like you have surrogates and Lee's my drawing surrogate. They're all stand-ins for you and that's Lee's role.

HUO: And why Lee?

ML: Because of the connections to *Drunken Bakers*. Because he draws for *Viz* and I like his style. It's very recognisably British. I like that.

HUO: This show at the Serpentine is a monographic show, it's about you by you, but you also undertake a lot of collaborations. We don't live in a time of movements anymore but more of moments but I still have the feeling that you are closely connected to art in this generation and also to the younger generation. Can you talk a little bit about that?

ML: About collaborating? Well with the band a lot of it came out of the Cabinet. Bonnie Camplin and Enrico David were both Cabinet artists.[2] And another person I collaborate a lot with is Martin McGeown from Cabinet, even though he won't acknowledge it. Like *Drunken Bakers*, Martin and I made that together. Collaboration, as far as I'm interested in it, is to do with your locality. It's to do with the people you're surrounded by and just working with them. It's not in terms of a movement, it's something more organic. I mean the thing with the Cabinet is that it's a very self-enclosed world and you have quite intense relationships with each other and if you're in an intense relationship with someone then you want to do things with them. It comes out of that intensity of friendship and interest in each other.

JPJ: In terms of intensity, your interest in science fiction, does that still hold true for you?

ML: I'm getting more interested in sci-fi. I like this thing I came across from the 1960s that's called Slipstream literature. It's not entirely science fiction but neither is it in any way realist. It's somewhere between the two. It looks at possibilities and those possibilities might be in the future but they are still realisable.

HUO: You recently curated magazine pages for *Artforum* – it's a visual essay, really. What is the role of curating in your practice?

ML: I don't really think of it as curating, it's just putting things together. I hope this doesn't sound pompous, which means that it will, but I'm not a curator I'm an essayist. I'm interested in making essays and the *Artforum* pages are a little essay about dumb things and the idea that you can talk to things that are dumb. In the same way *GreenScreenRefrigerator* is an essay about smart technology and *Fiorucci* is an essay about underground culture. They're all essays. I get interested in a thing and I make essays about it.

2. The band donAteller included Bonnie Camplin, Enrico David, Ed Liq and Leckey.

Concrete Vache

CONCRETE VACHE OR TEN YEARS OF EVENTS WITHIN A CONTEMPORARY BRITISH
ART GALLERY AS SCRIPTED BY ITSELF

INTERIOR: A GROUP OF TOWN PLANNERS & ARCHITECTS IN DISCUSSION

'What meaning does your construction have?' he asks,
'Where is the plan you are following, the blueprint?'
'We will show it to you as soon as the working day is over:
we cannot interrupt our work now,' they answer.
Work stops at sunset. Darkness falls over the building site.
The sky is filled with stars. 'There is the blueprint,' they say.

NARRATOR (V.O.)

MK G, Y2 K, the new millennium fast approaches but this only marks a moment. The stream
of life continues. Many have stayed, many have had children and they have stayed: the first
generation is becoming the second generation and the second generation is thinking about
a third generation. If one human year equals seven dog years, I would suggest that ten
human years equal one 'city year'. On that basis Milton Keynes is four years old.

So this is an attempt to capture the atmosphere of a classic British institution with
rudimentary pictures. Its formal qualities coincidentally referencing the gridded Master
plan of the host city; Milton Keynes. Not simply documents of places, they explore the
poetic and continuing possibility of private reflection. Images that represent the chaotic
forces of sex and money. The resulting work embodies a distinctive playfulness and
inquisitive curiosityinto the dynamics – architectural, spatial and aural – of the gallery,
town hall, factory, and bank.

INT. THE MIDDLE GALLERY

There are three rooms, each room has death very clearly and beauty very clearly. At the
end of a very long gallery, a sculpture, waves back. And the viewer is abducted.

A 'VACHE' ERA PAINTING OF RENE MAGRITTE APPEARS

'Louis meets a literary con man and says to him: 'Still got that pipe in your face!' 'I smoke
thirty a day' says the literary con man. Says Louis 'Yes, you are a great fuming heap.'

NARRATOR (V.O. Cont'd.)

This is an exploration of the possibility of seeing in the future, the images captured by our
eyes in the past. Proximity allows us to follow the artists thinking with greater immediacy.
When it comes to images he only has a non-productive, receptive organ, and when it comes
to something as complicated as telling a story by means of images, then his brain is simply
not constructed simplistically enough. Nothing but the primitive, undifferentiated, uncouth
'Here I am' of the picture.

ON HEADPHONES

You must push your head through the wall. It is not difficult to penetrate, for it is made of thin paper. But what is difficult is not to let oneself be deceived by the fact that there is already an extremely deceptive painting on the wall, showing you pushing your head through it. It tempts you to say, 'Am I not pushing through it all the time?'

NARRATOR (V.O Cont'd.)

Turn lies into speech, speech into nonsense, enemies into time and time into eternity. Eyelids, milky beans, a puddle, a leaning rail, a pruned tree adorned with snooker cue tips. Baptisms at sea, penguins in a zoo and the chrysalis-like forms of cast aluminium tents.Gathered and patterned, like compressed clusters on the body's inner landscape, or a sequence of echoes and reflections.

EXT. MIDSUMMER BOULEVARD

NARRATOR (V.O.)

Cracks in my body are filled with fine powder healed over. Objects, solid and considered, consider their possessions. Well designed, well put together. Objects are reduced to small filings, carbon monoxide and purple sparks. I will reduce possessions mechanically.

AN ASIDE

Rudiment or ru:dimant. 1. The elements or first principles of a subject. 2. An imperfect beginning of something undeveloped or yet to develop. 3. A part or organ imperfectly developed as being vestigial or having no function (e.g. the breast in males).

NARRATOR (V.O. Cont'd.)

Titles emit a charge. In their unashamed profusion they transgress all the usual boundaries, lead a wild life of their own and, like tropical twining plants, extend linguistic tendrils towards the pictures, now handing out obvious rhetorical advice, now addressing the viewer directly.

Titles, Women's tips for women:

1. Black silk underwear shines best if you wash it in black tea, not in water.
2. If you want to keep cucumbers fresh for a long time, give them one coat 'with thanks in advance.'
3. Sleep is an excellent beauty potion, known to humans and animals from their time as forest-dwellers.
4. Some things are recognised by the state for their importance.
5. Rub carpets with sauerkraut to freshen them up; lightly rub fine oil into worn out gramophone records.
6. You can prevent milk boiling over by putting a velvet insole into your shoe.

MUSIC FROM AN UNKNOWN SOURCE

Music from an unknown source: seal off the doors and do not enter the room. No sequence of tenses, no 'when,' no 'during,' no 'not only but also'.

'What's it actually about?'

QUESTIONER ONE

'What do you find inside your mouth?'

ANSWER

'I find the inside.'

QUESTIONER TWO

'And in the inside?'

ANSWER

'In the inside I find the morning.'

'Listen, your mouth is made for your ears.'

ALL

'Listen.'

NARRATOR (V.O.)

2004...La, la, la, la, la, la, la, la, la, la, la, la, la, la, la, la, la, la, la, la.

AN INFORMATION ANNOUNCEMENT

Thank you for your communication. You will be hearing from us shortly. You are not the only big shot around here. We are getting your range.

NARRATOR (V.O. Cont'd.)

Phantom compositions, a translucent plasticity of bodily form, in and out of the abstract and the solitariness of the urban hub. Misshapen anatomy with multiple perspectives, like the psychic chatter of instant electronic communication. This builds like a liquid intelligence, pushing peaks and troughs to give a bodily profile to our desires.

Time, Time spent with no specific intent, time as privilege, time without, time to explore, time to sit, time to stop, time to go beyond, time of pleasure, time limited by the heat of the day, time to change Berlin, time to imagine an ideal home, time to garden, time to find bad form, time to make a proper painting, time to lose in a field, time to construct a platform on which to stage. Time to occupy two chairs.

Possess, have exist, useful. Send out, develop, get rich, produce. Rise, promote, be promoted, revalue, go up. Gold, metal, money, golden, very rich, become. Fully grown, intent-ionally, success, complete. Silver, silver colour, money, very rich. Strive, exert effort, arouse.

A TAPE RECORDING

'...the container, if you want or the receptacle for...for how he plays. Which he, you know, recycles and picks upon...(UNINTELLIGIBLE)...for the Eagle. Which became the foundation for the museum. The actual objects are quite simple, or generic.'

INT. AT THE SURFACE OF A PAINTING

NARRATOR (V.O. TRANSLATES FROM THE FRENCH.)

Is this one a good painting...? Does it correspond with what you would expect from the most recent transformation which leads away from conceptual Art; to this, one could say, new version of a certain kind of figuration. And here are the various components of that landscape. The sky, the clouds, the sea, the mountain. This is a section from our key majestic view, where we attempt to settle our mind on the contemplation of the abstract world.

The image is an act of thought.

So I began with this picture. A vibrant word. Poppy red held within Breughel yellow. One hundred thousand pixels waving gently in the breeze. Sheer abundance is the only way, profusion, seduction, embranglement, toppling and falling, and the viewer's gaze is drawn by loops and knots.

EXT. THE PLAZA

Daily, the sculpture 'reinvents' itself, metamorphosing into infinitely varied configurations –

VOXPOP.

'I was thinking about maps.' 'I have cycled here.' 'Looking forward to the cinema later.' 'Will this automatic door open.'

NARRATOR (V.O. Cont'd.)

In such a way as to invite visitors to see how the works might 'speak' to each-other.

A figment beckons us – Click – 'Hey do you hear me?' – Click – 'I'm inside you' – Click – 'I'm yours' – Click.

...biding time...

RECORDING OF MICHAEL CRAIG-MARTIN IN THE BACKGROUND

NARRATOR (V.O. Cont'd.)

This is a machine for performing in; a soft machine, warmed by hand-rendered and hand-polished finishes, enlivened by the choice of an Yves Klein-inspired colour scheme – deep blue, red and gold. One object is as good as another, one colour is as good as another colour, some girl's mothers are bigger than other girl's mothers. And this is because the machine is a programme...and it makes all the decisions.

Person to Person, People to People, two worlds are projected alongside one another: the world as it is, and the world as it could be. The intention of the work is an attempt to find a meta-world that can bridge the two contexts. In order to 'find' this 'meta-world', one of two kinds of transformations has to occur, either in the way we think about our world, i.e. our perception of it, or in the world itself. Within every person there lies the transformer and the initiation of transformations is essential to each individual.

At the end, nothing of the intervention remains; the materials are cleared away, the original space is returned to its former self and all that remains, is photographic evidence and memory.

Mark Leckey and Martin McGeown

All words from Milton Keynes Gallery Archive; press releases, catalogues, reviews etc.

Concrete Vache, 2010

Concrete Vache, 2010

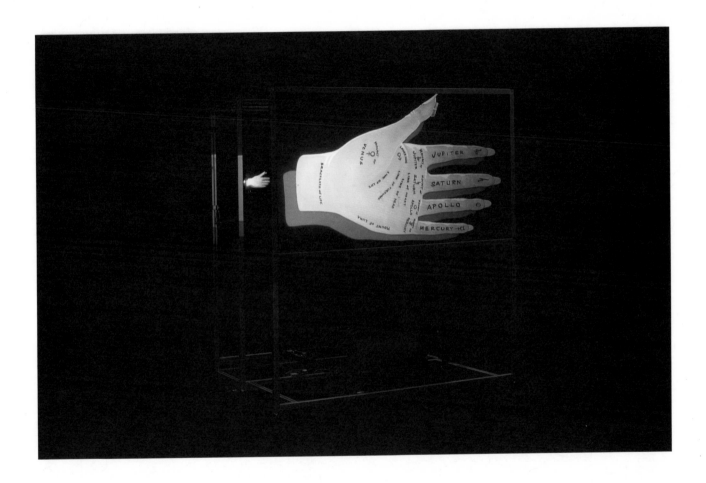

Concrete Vache, 2010

Concrete Vache, 2010

GreenScreenRefrigeratorAction

GreenScreenRefrigeratorAction, 2010

NUKE THE FRIDGE

My heart beats, electrically
My brain computes, programme me
I am complicated, let me be
I am you, programme me[1]

In 1959, US President Richard Nixon and Soviet Premier Nikita Khrushchev famously held their 'Kitchen Debate', in which they competed on their common accomplishments in industrial consumerism. Their cybernetic faith in scenario-planning begat today's confidence in systems rather than agents, in technologies rather than people.[2] Planners gave birth to imaginary futures in which people were liberated and fulfilled by new technological developments and in which the current socio-economic system not only delivered but triumphed. The refrigerator and the race to the moon were two sides of the same coin – attempts to sanitise military technology designed to 'dematerialise' us. The fridge kept our milk fresh for longer, but it couldn't save us; rather, it was hurtling us faster towards Armageddon.

Now, once again, the humble fridge is at the forefront of technocratic foresight. Smart fridges use radio frequency identification (RFID) to encourage new forms of consumer-free consumerism, reading and writing implants in food products as they enter their cool ambience. Where Nixon and Khrushchev worried about how to ensure the even provision of manufactured products, today's transnationalists, such as the European Union, are fixated on delivering microeconomic access to 'services'. This means overcoming the digital divide by rolling out an ambient infrastructure that is dematerialised and ubiquitous; one led by today's techno-social interactionism rather than by 1950s-style retail-acceptance.

'Every vehicle is a node, every good is tagged.'[3]

Our ambient intelligence (AmI) is driven not just by biotech convergence such as in RFID nanosurgical 'wetware', but by cultural convergence as ever faster and denser social synergies are enabled by the resonance of the networked body. Ambient culture has the immense potential to connect people in ways that can significantly expand the sensorium. Just as humans and animals form a continuum, the 'social' and 'technological' spheres converge as symbiotic complex systems. So AmI can be, in theory at least, related to our desires. AmI 'thinks' for us. We ask it to create environments calibrated and 'mass-customised'[4] to our needs. This is where ambience comes in. Smart fridges are ambient in as much as we are no longer supposed to notice them.[5] Like the air in the room, they are just 'everyware',[6] quietly procuring an experience-centred mash-up of goods, ideas and services.

1. Bruce Clinton Haack, 'Programme Me', *The Electric Lucifer*, Columbia Records, 1970.
2. 'But in the 1950s (and in many ways, today) it was an elitist model of change that counted "the people" only as epiphenomena of some feedback loop initiated further up the hierarchy of power and/or colonialism, an artefact of an altogether more technocratic age.' Samuel Gerald Collins,

'Margaret Mead Answers', *All Tomorrow's Cultures: Anthropological Engagements with the Future* (New York: Berghahn Books, 2008), p. 31.
3. K. Ducatel, M. Bogdanowicz, F. Scapolo, J. Leijten and J-C. Burgelman, *Scenarios for Ambient Intelligence in 2010*, Institute for Prospective Technological Studies, Joint Research Centre, European Commission, Seville, 2001, p. 41.

4. J. Pine II, *Mass Customization: The New Frontier in Business Competition*, (Boston: Harvard Business School, 1992).
5. For example, see Tim O'Reilly's concept of Web 3.0, a 'sensor-driven collective intelligence', or Mark Weisser's 'ubiquitous computing'.
6. A. Greenfield, *Everyware: The Dawning Age of Ubiquitous Computing* (Berkeley, CA: New Riders Publishing, 2006).

What is crucial here is to notice how we are forgetting how to notice. Since the 1950s, owning a TV has meant buying the advertising they carry. We can turn the TV down, over or off, but short of throwing it away, we can't wholly escape the ads. TVs are not smart or interactive; they belong to a broadcasting era that's past its sell-by date. The smart fridge is a new breed of media that is rapidly replacing broadcasting; radio enabled, it heralds narrowcasting by stealth. TV shows are just a distraction from the ads. Of course the ads are a distraction to us, so it's best that they circumvent this line of communication altogether. Smartwear enhances brand loyalty by cutting out the middlemen (the broadcasters and consumers), allowing brands and distributors to pitch directly to our fridges.

Fully immersive convenience technology is emotional, viral and hypnotic. It radically extends the avant-garde's preoccupation with secular transubstantiation, with 'data aura', with the object as Host. Where modern technocratic culture was driven by systems and structures, our ambient ecology is driven by textures. And so we are falling in love again with our fridges. They nurture and suckle, intuitively providing us with what we think we want. The smart fridge caresses our membrane, making it as porous as a network gateway is permeable, allowing information to flow out of as well as into the skin. Will the smart fridge return our love? Will it always be faithful to our desires? What are the chances that this affair is in fact a 'consciousness' determined by a network of investors?

This dystopic future-present of a techno-enhanced 'experience economy' resonates and builds like radio interference. Every 'thing' becomes a form of medium that makes everyone's voice available (but not necessarily heard); all that is solid is vacuumed into the semantic web of liminal interference. There is no public or private, no inside or outside, no virtual or real. A cacophony of objects, images, sounds and data are converged invisibly, inconspicuously, into a singular, mythical, black box embedded in our heads. This prospective singularity is a product of behaviour that we have cultivated since the growth of the web in mid-1990s. As a means to curate information, convergence tech fights fire with fire, overcoming the noise of the traffic by pumping up the volume on the TV. Ambient soronity is a black hole: the louder it gets the more attractive its magnetism; it has no respite. A virtual vampiric consumer of consumerism, will the fridge eat itself?

We can't know how ambient culture will play out and we have no means of visualising its pulse. Since ambient culture is not optical nor material, it is not an empirical question of what an emerging ambient ecology will look like, but rather of how it will feel. Ambience is a field not a form; its manifestation is imperceptible. We need to figure out how and when to turn the dial, which fader to push in which direction. If all culture occupies the same terrain and is thus a form of tangential interference, what makes some of it ambient is its tactical lateralness, its bespoke stealth, its unpredictability. As Mark Leckey's *GreenScreenRefrigeratorAction*, 2010, uniquely demonstrates, this is a question of performance. The ambient field is to be played like an instrument.

Ambient culture promises to be experience-centred; the question is whether or not the kind of experiences valued and nurtured will be genuinely holistic and embodied. It is up to us to determine the outcome of this battle for our homes, our bodies and our minds. We might want to start by having a few words with our refrigerators.

Neil Mulholland

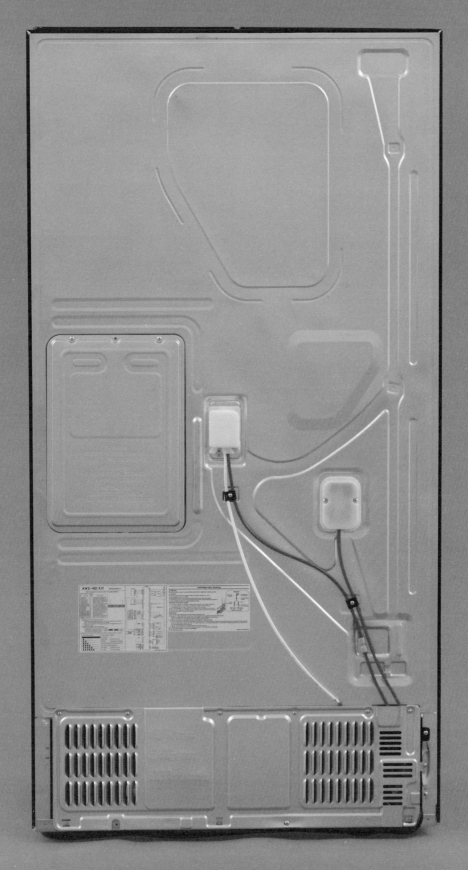

GreenScreenRefrigerator, 2010 (open)

Produce in freezer

Pueraria montana var. lobata (common name: kudzu or vine-a-minute)

Heat exchange diagram (Samsung RFG293HABP Bottom Freezer French Door Refrigerator)

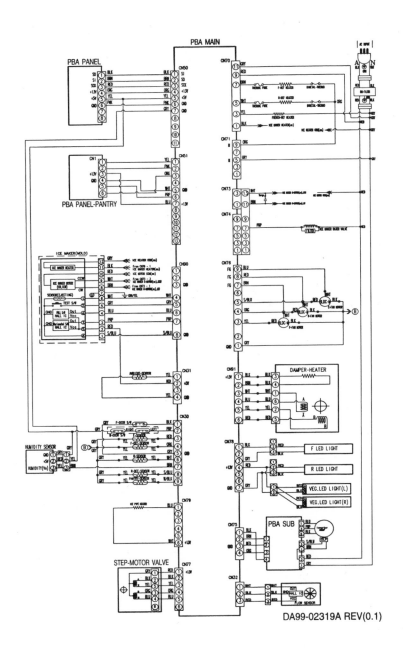

DA99-02319A REV(0.1)

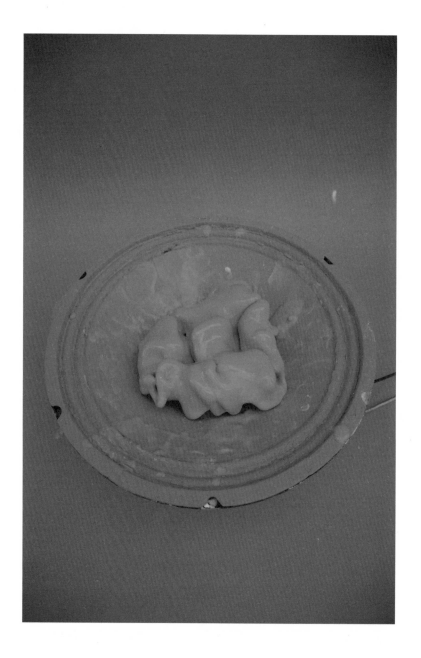

NON-NEWTONIANS

Err, tails, lots of tails, recurring tails. Moving tendrils, many headed cephalopods. I might
call it err...tentacled, colloidal, semi-amorphous, partly squamous and partly rugose-ugh!
With what can only be described as promiscuous intent they seem to be caressing each
other, enthusiastically touching, embracing themselves – them self...itself! Errm, Their
arms – or whatever you'd call them – these reticulose pseudopedia-raised, reaching up
to whatever lies tantalizingly out of frame as they move hap-haptically to the ant music on
the stereo. Writhing up from their fluidizing bed as they flutter like in time-lapse, a cinematic
blossoming of life (like) towards a light they cannot see but can hear and feel like they
possess an awareness in which the music is the electric soil in which this seminal-semolina?
– stuff could emerge out of...a simple spontaneous arising, auto-erotic, non-living newborn
without a mother – you've got to be fucking kidding! What is this thing? This, this cornstarch
encounter group, this nameless yeast achieving consciousness or consciousnesses, a wet
cheese in a delirium? a self-organising biotic yogurt, a voluptuous living custard!

Mark Leckey

BigBoxStatueAction, 2003–11
Sound System 'in conversation' with
Henry Moore's *Upright Motive No. 9*:

   Sound System, 2003
   4 low range speakers, 2 mid range
   speakers, 3 high range speakers,
   1 wooden sound buffer, 4 amplifiers,
   1 equalizer, 1 stereo/mono crossover,
   1 mixer, 1 DVD player, cables
   Dimensions variable
   Fondation Louis Vuitton pour la création

   Henry Moore, *Upright Motive No. 9*, 1979
   Bronze
   Height 335.5 cm
   The Henry Moore Foundation

GreenScreenRefrigeratorAction, 2010–11
QuickTime movie, 20 min, Green Screen
Infinity Cove, Samsung RFG293HABP
Bottom Freezer French Door Refrigerator,
2 Samsung 58″ screens, 2 Samsung Galaxy
S Mobile Phones, 2 Samsung Galaxy Tabs,
1 Samsung Printer
Courtesy of the artist and Gavin Brown's
enterprise, New York

Fiorucci Made Me Hardcore, 1999
VHS transferred to QuickTime, 15 min
Courtesy of the artist, Gavin Brown's
enterprise, New York, Galerie Daniel
Buchholz, Cologne and Cabinet Gallery,
London

Sound System, 2003
Hi-tech audio equipment
Dimensions variable
Collection Charles Asprey

Dubplate (Sound System 1), 2001
Sound system, 2 amplifiers, record player,
acetate record
Dimensions variable
Boros Collection, Berlin

TRAILER FOR SEE, WE ASSEMBLE, 2011
QuickTime movie
Courtesy of the artist

RFG293H, 2010
Silkscreen on matt board
208.5 × 138 cm
Courtesy of the artist

BIOGRAPHY

1964
Born in Birkenhead, UK

1990
BA Newcastle Polytechnic, UK

Lives and works in London

SELECTED SOLO EXHIBITIONS

2010
GreenScreenRefrigeratorAction, Gavin Brown's enterprise, New York
Concrete Vache, Cabinet Gallery, London
The Life and Times of Milton Keynes Gallery, Milton Keynes Gallery (co-curated with Martin McGeown)

2009
Mark Leckey in the Long Tail, Abrons Arts Center, New York, presented by the Museum of Modern Art
and possibly but not certainly Mark Leckey and Frances Stark, Galerie Daniel Buchholz, Berlin

2008
Cinema-in-the-Round, Guggenheim Museum, New York, presented by Creative Time
Resident, Kölnischer Kunstverein, Cologne

2007
Industrial Light & Magic, Le Consortium, Dijon
Dead or Alive, Galerie Daniel Buchholz, Cologne

2006
Drunken Bakers, Passerby, New York
Mark Leckey, Gavin Brown's enterprise, New York

2005
Gorgeousness & Gorgeosity, Portikus im Leinwandhaus, Frankfurt am Main
Mark Leckey, Cabinet Gallery, London

2004
Septic Tank, Gavin Brown's enterprise, New York
Parade, Cabinet Gallery, London
Sound System, Mercer Union, Toronto

2003
Mark Leckey, Migros Museum, Zurich, Switzerland
Dubplate, Locust Projects, Miami
BigBoxStatueAction, Tate Britain, London

2002
Sound System, Gavin Brown's enterprise, New York
Fiorucci Made Me Hardcore, Santa Monica Museum of Art, USA

2000
London, My Part in its Downfall, Galerie Daniel Buchholz, Cologne
Fiorucci Made Me Hardcore, Gavin Brown's enterprise, New York

1994
The Model, Gavin Brown's enterprise, San Francisco

SELECTED GROUP EXHIBITIONS

2011
Push and Pull, Tate Modern, London

2010
10,000 Lives: The Eighth Gwangju Biennale, South Korea
Moving Images: Artists & Video/Film, Museum Ludwig, Cologne

2009
Beg Borrow and Steal, Rubell Family Collection, Miami
Playing Homage, Vancouver Contemporary Art Gallery, Canada
Dispersion, Institute of Contemporary Arts, London

2008
Turner Prize 2008, Tate Britain, London
Tarantula, Fondazione Nicola Trussardi, Milan
Egypted, Kunsthalle Exnergasse, Vienna

2007
Sympathy for the Devil, Museum of Contemporary Art, Chicago
Sound of Music, Broelmuseum, Kortrijk, Belgium
Pale Carnage, Arnolfini, Bristol

2006
Defamation of Character, PS1 Contemporary Art Center, New York
Music is a Better Noise, PS1 Contemporary Art Center, New York
Tate Triennial of Contemporary British Art, Tate Britain, London
Music for People, Dundee Contemporary Arts, UK

2005
Istanbul, 9th Istanbul Biennial, Turkey
British Art Show 6, BALTIC Centre for Contemporary Art, Gateshead, UK (a Hayward Gallery touring exhibition, travelled to Manchester, Nottingham, and Bristol)

2004
Faces in the Crowd, Castello di Rivoli, Turin, Italy and Whitechapel, London
Manifesta 5, European Biennial of Contemporary Art, San Sebastian, Spain

2003
Fast Forward, ZKM, Karlsruhe, Germany
Inaugural Exhibition, Gavin Brown's enterprise, New York
Sound Systems, Salzburger Kunstverein, Austria
Objekte in Ton (Arbeitstitel), Salzburger Kunstverein, Austria
Il Quarto Sesso, Stazione Leopolda, Florence, Italy
Mixtape, CCA Wattis Institute for Contemporary Arts, San Francisco
The Fourth Sex: The Extreme People of Adolescence, Pitti Immagine, Florence, Italy
Electric Dreams, Barbican Art Gallery, London
Remix, Tate Liverpool, UK
Contemporary Art and Pop, Tate Liverpool, UK
Three Videos, Low Gallery, Los Angeles
Shoot the Singer: Music on Video, Institute of Contemporary Art, Philadelphia

2001
Le Printemps de Septembre, festival of contemporary art, Toulouse, France
Brown, The Approach, London
Century City, Tate Modern, London
Sound and Vision, Institute of Contemporary Arts, London

2000
Protest & Survive, Whitechapel Gallery, London
Discovery, Pitti Immagine, Florence, Italy

1999
Village Disco, Cabinet Gallery, London
Crash, Institute of Contemporary Arts, London

1996
Gavin Brown's enterprise, New York

1994
Gavin Brown's enterprise, New York

1990
New Contemporaries, Institute of Contemporary Arts, London

Elena Bonanno di Linguaglossa
The Hon. Alexander Brennan
Ben Bridgewater
James and Felicia Brocklebank
Chris Byrne
William Burlington
Jessica Carlisle
C. Cartellieri
Antony Clavel and Maria Novella Vecere
Patrick C. Cunningham
Indi Davis
Suzanne Egeran
Sara Farah
Roxanna Farboud
Mrs Selma Feriani
Mrs Deana Goldstein
Marie Guerlain
Michael Hadjedj
Mr S. Haq
Matt Hermer
Carolyn Hodler
Nicholas W. Hofgren
Julia Hofmann
Olivia Howell and Michael Patterson
Karim Jallad
Zoe Karafylakis Sperling
Chloe Kinsman
John Krasner
Niels Kroner
Georgina and Alastair Laing
Mans Larsson
Maged Latif
Arianne Levene
James Lindon
Dan Lywood
Jean-David Malat
Marina Marini
Jose Mazoy
Anne Mellentin
John Paul Micalleff
Laura Modiano
Fernando J. Moncho Lobo
Sheryl Needham
Isabelle Nowak and Torsten Winkler
David Olsson
Samira Parkinson-Smith
Catherine Patha
Anja Pauls
Julia Pincus
Carlos and Francesca Pinto
Harry Plotnick
Julia Prestia
Mike Radcliffe
Farah Rahim Ismail
Laurent Rappaport
Piotr Rejmer
Alexandra Ritterman
Claudia Ruimy
Poppy Sebire
Xandi Schemann
Alyssa Sherman
Tammy Smulders
Christopher Thomsen
Jonathan Tyler
Andy Valmorbida

Mr and Mrs Vincent Van Heyste
Rachel Verghis
Sam Waley-Cohen
Trent Ward
Lucy Wood
Omar Giovanni Zaghis
Mr and Mrs Nabil Zaouk
Fabrizio D. Zappaterra

BENEFACTORS
Mr and Mrs Allahyar Afshar
Shane Akeroyd
Mr Niklas Antman and Miss Lisa Almen
Paul and Kia Armstrong
Jane Attias
Anne Best and Roddy Kinkead-Weekes
Roger and Beverley Bevan
Anthony and Gisela Bloom
Mr and Mrs John Botts
Marcus Boyle
Mervyn and Helen Bradlow
Vanessa Branson
Benjamin Brown
Ed Burstell
Mrs Tita Granda Byrne
Lavinia Calza Beveridge
Azia Chatila
Paul Clifford
Sadie Coles
Carole and Neville Conrad
Matthew Conrad
Gul Coskun
Yasmine Datnow
Mr and Mrs Colin David
Mr and Mrs Christopher Didizian
Robin and Noelle Doumar
Mike Fairbrass
Mr and Mrs Mark Fenwick
John Ferreira
Hako and Dörte, Graf and Gräfin
   von Finckenstein
David and Jane Fletcher
Eric and Louise Franck
Alan and Joanna Gemes
Zak and Candida Gertler
Leonardo and Alessia Giangreco
Hugh Gibson
Peter Gidal
David Gill
Dimitri J. Goulandris
Richard and Judith Greer
Linda and Richard Grosse
Louise Hallett
Liz Hammond
Jeremy Hargreave
Susan Harris
Timothy and Daška Hatton
Maria and Stratis Hatzistefanis
Alison Henry-Davies
Mrs Christine Johnston
Marcelle Joseph and Paolo Cicchiné
Jennifer Kersis
James and Clare Kirkman
Mr and Mrs Lahoud
Geraldine Larkin

Sydney Levinson
George and Angie Loudon
Sotiris T.F. Lyritzis
Mr Otto Julius Maier and
   Mrs Michèle Claudel-Maier
Cary J. Martin
Mr and Mrs Stephen Mather
Ruth and Robert Maxted
Viviane and James Mayor
Warren and Victoria Miro
Gillian Mosely
Dr Maigaelle Moulene
Georgia Oetker
Tamiko Onozawa
Teresa Oulton
Desmond Page and Asun Gelardin
Maureen Paley
Dominic Palfreyman
Midge and Simon Palley
Julia Peyton-Jones OBE
Sophie Price
Mathew Prichard
Mrs Janaki Prosdocimi
Ashraf Qizilbash
Bruce and Shadi Ritchie
Kasia Robinski
Kimberley Robson-Ortiz
Jacqueline and Nicholas Roe
Fabio Rossi
Victoria, Lady de Rothschild
James Roundell and Bona Montagu
Michael and Julia Samuel
Ronnie and Vidal Sassoon
Joana and Henrik Schliemann
Nick Simou and Julie Gatland
Bina and Philippe von Stauffenberg
Tanya and David Steyn
Simone and Robert Suss
The Thames Wharf Charity
Britt Tidelius
Gretchen and Jus Trusted
Audrey Wallrock
Lady Corinne Wellesley
Alannah Weston
Helen Ytuarte White
Dr Yvonne Winkler
Mr Ulf Wissen
Henry and Rachel Wyndham
Mr and Mrs Nabil Zaouk

And Patrons, Future Contemporaries
and Benefactors who wish to remain
anonymous

SUPPORTED BY
Arts Council England
The Royal Parks
Westminster City Council

This catalogue is published on the occasion of the exhibition Mark Leckey: *SEE, WE ASSEMBLE* at the Serpentine Gallery, London, 19 May – 26 June 2011.

Exhibition curated by

Julia Peyton-Jones
Director, Serpentine Gallery
and Co-Director, Exhibition and
Programmes

Hans Ulrich Obrist
Co-Director, Exhibition and
Programmes and Director,
International Projects

Kathryn Rattee
Curator

The exhibition is made possible by

with the generous support of the
Mark Leckey Exhibition Circle

Marlon Abela, Morton's Club
Charles Asprey
Galerie Daniel Buchholz, Berlin/Köln
Gavin Brown's enterprise
and those who wish to remain anonymous

Media Partner

THE
INDEPENDENT

The Serpentine Gallery is supported by

The artist would like to thank:
Lizzie Carey-Thomas for de-machining me; James Mullord for his mechanical mastery; Tim Bacon for all the CG brilliance; Mark Blower for his photographic abilities; Rainer Usselman for the happy finish on the Moore poster; Kathryn Rattee for her curatorial nous; Martin McGeown & Andrew Wheatley; Gavin Brown; Christopher Müller & Daniel Buchholz; Charles Asprey; Mike Gaughan; Kelly Taylor for GreenScreen in New York; Julia Peyton-Jones and Hans Ulrich Obrist for the opportunity; Catherine Wood, Neil Mulholland and Simon Reynolds for their essays; Freddie, Patricia and everyone else who has helped me out.

Serpentine Gallery

Kensington Gardens
London W2 3XA
T +44 (0)20 7402 6075
F +44 (0)20 7402 4103
www.serpentinegallery.org

Koenig Books Ltd
At the Serpentine Gallery
Kensington Gardens
London W2 3XA
www.koenigbooks.co.uk

Distribution:
Buchhandlung Walther König, Köln
Ehrenstr. 4, 50672 Köln
T +49 (0) 221 / 20 59 6-53
F +49 (0) 221 / 20 59 6-60
verlag@buchhandlung-walther-koenig.de

Switzerland:
AVA Verlagsauslieferungen AG
Centralweg 16
CH-8910 Affoltern a.A.
T +41 (44) 762 42 00
F +41 (44) 762 42 10
verlagsservice@ava.ch

UK & Eire:
Cornerhouse Publications
70 Oxford Street
Manchester M1 5NH
T +44 (0) 161 200 15 03
F +44 (0) 161 200 15 04
publications@cornerhouse.org

Outside Europe:
D.A.P. / Distributed Art Publishers, Inc.
155 6th Avenue, 2nd Floor
New York, NY 10013
T +1 212-627-1999
F +1 212-627-9484
eleshowitz@dapinc.com

ISBN 978-3-86335-039-0
(Koenig Books, London)

ISBN 978-1-905190-41-6
(Serpentine Gallery, London)

Edited by
Kathryn Rattee and Melissa Larner

Designed by
Fraser Muggeridge studio

Printed in the UK